How
DID THEY
MISS IT?

Antoinette Greenidge and Alicia Hurtt

Copyright © 2024
Antoinette Greenidge and Alicia Hurtt

Published by:
Cole & Co Publishing House
6720 E. Fowler Ave, Suite 161
Tampa, FL 33617

All rights reserved.
No portion of this book may be reproduced,
photocopied, stored, or transmitted in
any form-except by prior approval of publisher.

A MESSAGE FROM THE AUTHOR, ANTOINETTE GREENIDGE

Scan the QR code below to view her videos.

IN LOVING MEMORY OF
ANTOINETTE GREENIDGE

DOB 8/30/1962 *DOT 06/07/2023*

From all of us to our dear sister Antoinette,
We love you for always being you!
We love you for maintaining the peace! You were our peacemaker!

We love you for your jovial personality!
We love you for always being a giver of yourself,
your time, your resources, and your love!
We love you for understanding us all individually; you never judged us, you were very open, and we could talk to you about anything at any time. You were our angel on earth!
You will truly be missed by all of us!

Say hello to Adrianna, Grandma Ursula, and Mom for us!
Love Always,
Andrea, Anna, Anthony, Arnold, and Arlene

In Loving Memory of Antoinette Greenidge

POEM:

I know my heart is in there...

I know my heart is in there

I can feel it

Or maybe I can

I think it's here

I think it may be there

No, it's with you

Its always been with you

You gave it to me

You called me

You desired me

And God gave me to you

A piece of you

Its there

Or maybe it's not

I know it is

In Loving Memory of Antoinette Greenidge

I will always and forever know it

I will always cherish it

I will always embrace it

I will always value it

It lives on

It lives on in me

It lives on in you

It has been given to many that are not aware, but I know

God knows

And my children and their children will, too

I will always love you…. I found my heart.

POEM 2:

Are you giving up...

Are you giving up?

Giving up on me

Giving up on us

Giving up on you

Our life

Your life

The good times

The bad times

All the laughter

All the joy

All the experiences

All the adventures

Are you giving up?

Giving up on me

Giving up on us

Giving up on you

In Loving Memory of Antoinette Greenidge

What about that trip?

What about that recipe?

What about that show?

What about just sitting and talking about nothing together?

Are you giving up?

Giving up on me

Giving up on us

Giving up on you

No, you are set free!

You have done your work!

You have been given the ultimate promotion!

I don't understand sometimes!

I don't want to be without physically, but I know God wants you more, and he will take good care

of me so you can enjoy your forever.

Thank you for not giving up on us

Thank you for not giving up on you

Thank you for not giving up on me

Love, Alicia

TRIBUTE TO MY MOM

Ma, you taught me to conquer my fears and try again. You also taught me that loneliness doesn't mean I am ever alone. I must remember to call on Jesus, my Savior! Now it's my turn to fight for Jesus, learn more and teach more, and it's my turn to 'be.' I explored new places and tried new things because, as you would tell me, "What's the worst that can happen?" You have to start over again.? Well, get started all over again. In Jesus' almighty name!" I will forever remember our talks and your wild sayings. "Hide ur kids, hide ur wife," just for laughs. And Ma, laughter was always the best medicine. I am thankful you blessed me with the parenting you gave me, and I'm honored to have made you laugh so hard. This is not Goodbye; this is see you later when it's my turn to rejoice in His presence!

Love your last Baby,
Jace Amelia Greenidge

How Did They Miss It?

Tribute to My Mom

TABLE OF CONTENTS

A Message From the Author, Antonette Greenidge iii

In Loving Memory of Antoinette Greenidge v

Tribute to My Mom xiii

Table of Contents xvii

A Girl from Trinidad: Roots and Early Blossoms 1

In DC, Now What 5

A Love Story 9

Work Hard 13

Kids Will Be Kids 27

A Faithful Servant 33

How Did They Miss It? 47

Favorite Songs and Hymns of Comfort 85

Prayers 89

Scriptures of Encouragement and Healing 99

Living the Beatitudes (Matthew 5:2-12):
Antoinette's Inspirational Journey of Faithful Service. 109

Contact 114

A GIRL FROM TRINIDAD: ROOTS AND EARLY BLOSSOMS

Antoinette Greendige, a soul born on August 30, 1962, at the San Juan, Port of Spain General Hospital in Trinidad and Tobago, emerged into the world as a radiant blossom in a tapestry woven by Harold Joseph, Annette Phillip, and stepfather Arnim Pritchard. Raised amid the warm embrace of family, Antoinette shared the dance of childhood with six siblings—Andrinna (whose memory lingered in the family's heart), Andrea, Anna, Anthony, Arlene, and Arnold.

From her earliest years, Antoinette displayed a spirited independence and a vivid imagination, setting the stage for a life marked by resilience and creativity. Her entrepreneurial spark ignited early, as she learned the art of crafting Tambourines from her mother, Annette. What began as a childhood pastime evolved into a showcase of resourcefulness and business acumen as Antoinette ventured into the world of commerce, selling her handcrafted Tambourines at school. While her siblings freely spent their earnings, Antoinette embraced a different path—saving diligently, sharing generously, and finding joy in responsibility and leisure.

Antoinette's educational journey unfolded at Morvent Central for Elementary School in Trinidad and Tobago, where her academic prowess shone bright enough to secure success in the common entrance exam. As life took a transformative turn, she found herself under the nurturing wings of her grandparents, Ursula and Henry Skeete. The journey across oceans led her to the United States of America, where she established her new home in Tyler House, Northeast Washington, D.C.

Within the vibrant halls of Marva Washington and Carol Jr High School, Antoinette continued to showcase her multifaceted talents. Her grace and charisma earned her the title of 1st runner-up in the school's beauty pageant, a testament to her inner and outer beauty. Beyond the allure of pageantry, Antoinette dedicated her time to a cause close to her heart—volunteering as a candy striper at Providence Hospital. In the corridors of healing, she found fulfillment in supporting staff and patients, a foreshadowing of her future in the healthcare profession.

Responsibility became a cornerstone of Antoinette's character, a trait instilled by her grandmother, Ursula. Diligently completing daily chores, she embraced each task with a sense of duty that would become a defining feature of her adult life. In the nurturing environment of Tyler House, under the watchful eyes of Ursula and Henry Skeete, Antoinette's roots began to intertwine with the soil of her newfound home, setting the stage for the remarkable journey that would follow.

As we delve into the early chapters of Antoinette's life, we witness the seeds of resilience, responsibility, and compassion taking root in the fertile soil of her upbringing. The stage is set for the bloom of a life that would touch the hearts of many and leave an indelible mark on the world.

IN DC, NOW WHAT

The tapestry of Antoinette's life was woven with threads of resilience, courage, and grace as she embarked on a transformative journey from her childhood home in Trinidad to the bustling cityscape of Washington, D.C. Navigating this new environment with the weight of responsibility on her shoulders, Antoinette's story is a testament to her unwavering spirit, her dedication to family, and her pursuit of personal passions.

A New Beginning in a New Land:

Antoinette's early childhood was spent on the vibrant island of Trinidad, where the tropical rhythms of life shaped her experiences. But destiny beckoned her to a new chapter in a distant land. As a young immigrant arriving in Washington, D.C., the city's towering monuments and bustling streets starkly contrasted her island home. Amid the unfamiliarity, Antoinette embarked on a journey of adaptation, embracing the challenges and opportunities ahead.

A Family United, Yet Separated:

Separated from her mother, who remained in Trinidad, Antoinette found solace in her grandparents' loving embrace. Under their guidance, she discovered the strength within her to shoulder responsibilities beyond her years. Balancing schoolwork with household chores became second nature, as she fulfilled her duties with purpose and commitment. This early exposure to responsibilities forged her character and laid the foundation for the remarkable woman she would become.

The Encouragement of a Grandfather's Wisdom:

Antoinette's grandfather, recognizing the remarkable qualities within her, played a pivotal role in shaping her destiny. With quiet wisdom and deep understanding, he encouraged her to explore her passions and talents. He saw her grace, her determination, and her quiet strength. Inspired by his guidance, Antoinette embarked on a journey of self-discovery that would lead her to unexpected avenues of growth and fulfillment.

Pursuing Passion and Compassion:

In the corridors of a local hospital, Antoinette found a space where her passion for dance merged with her compassionate heart.

Volunteering as a candy striper, she brought joy to patients and a gentle touch to their healing journey. Through her service, she discovered the profound impact of caring for others, a lesson that would later shape her career in healthcare.

Facing Challenges with Grace:

In a new school environment, Antoinette encountered the trials that often accompany being different. She faced teasing and questioning, but her gentle spirit remained steadfast. Rather than allowing negativity to define her, she embraced her uniqueness and chose to be true to herself. Her unwavering authenticity drew others to her, as they recognized the beauty of her character beyond external appearances.

Antoinette's journey from Trinidad to Washington, D.C., was more than a physical relocation; it transformed her heart and soul. Through challenges and triumphs, she navigated the path with a blend of grace and determination that characterized her every step. Her story reminds us that embracing change, shouldering responsibilities, and pursuing our passions can shape us into resilient individuals capable of creating meaningful connections and leaving indelible marks on the lives we touch. Antoinette's journey from an immigrant child to a compassionate healthcare professional is an inspiring testament to the power of inner strength, embracing new horizons, and the beauty of being authentically oneself.

A LOVE STORY

Within the walls of the Tyler House, a tapestry of love and fate unfolded, weaving together the destinies of Antoinette Greenidge and Dave Greenidge in a narrative that would resonate through the annals of time. Their love story, akin to a symphony composed by destiny itself, began as a quiet melody that slowly crescendoed through the interconnected threads of friendships and familial bonds.

Dave, drawn to Antoinette's spirit like a moth to a flame, embarked on a journey of love that demanded diligence and heartfelt pursuit. The mosaic of Tyler House witnessed his patient endeavors to win her heart, each effort a note in the symphony of their burgeoning courtship. Antoinette, with her vibrant spirit, became the muse that inspired Dave's melodies, and in the intricate dance of courtship, they discovered a harmonious blend of companionship and understanding.

Antoinette, however, played hard to get, a playful dance of resistance that tested the depths of Dave's commitment. Despite the challenges and the elusive nature of her heart, Dave remained steadfast and diligent. He embraced the dance, matching her steps with unwavering determination. Each step and gesture became a testament to his love and the unyielding belief that Antoinette was the one he was destined to share his life with.

The crescendo of their courtship led to a momentous climax when, after a year of shared dreams and whispered promises, they stood together to exchange vows—a sacred covenant that would bind them through the highs and lows of life. The young couple, armed with love and determination, settled into an apartment nestled in the heartbeat of the city, ready to embark on a journey that would unfurl over the canvas of time.

From the sanctity of their union, a family tree blossomed, each branch adorned with the names of their cherished offspring. Alicia, Angela, and Jace became the living embodiment of their love, and a serendipitous blessing in the form of Lil Dave graced their lives—a bonus son who added an extra layer of joy to their familial tapestry. The circle of their love expanded further as grandchildren—Alajah,

Anastasia, Amara, Anne, Aubrey, Daryl Jr., and Chase—brought laughter, warmth, and abundant joy into their lives.

As the pages of their love story turned, July beckoned as a month of profound significance. It would have been a milestone—a commemoration of 40 years of marriage, a testament to a love that endured the tests of time. In the quiet moments of reflection, Antoinette's presence lingered as more than just the love of Dave's life. She was the very heartbeat that resonated through the chambers of his heart—a timeless melody that played on, creating an eternal soundtrack of cherished memories.

Their love, forged through the crucible of time and the dance of persistence, stood as a testament to resilience, understanding, and unwavering commitment. In the garden of their shared experiences, they nurtured a marriage and a legacy of enduring love that would be passed down through the generations. Antoinette, in her role as mother and grandmother, became a lighthouse of love, guiding, cherishing, and adoring each member of her expanding family.

The story of Antoinette and Dave—a love story etched in time, ties that bind, and the dance of persistence—continues to unfold, leaving an indelible mark on the hearts of those who witness its beauty. Through the tapestry of their shared moments, the threads of love and commitment intertwine, creating a legacy that transcends the boundaries of earthly existence, forever echoing in the corridors of familial bonds and enduring affection.

WORK HARD

In the vast tapestry of human history, the medical field stands as a towering testament to the indomitable strength of the human spirit, showcasing the lengths individuals are willing to go to alleviate suffering and bring solace to the afflicted. At the heart of this intricate mosaic is Antoinette Greendige, a name that resounds with unwavering dedication and boundless compassion. With over a quarter-century committed to the medical field, her roles ranging from nursing assistant and CNA to LPN, Greendige's journey epitomizes the intricate paradox of a path that is both thankless and yet profoundly self-rewarding.

The Barren Desert of Recognition:

In a world clamoring for acknowledgment, the medical field can often seem like a barren desert where the rains of gratitude rarely fall. Healthcare professionals, though they stand at the forefront of healing and compassion, often find themselves navigating the arid expanse of underappreciation. However, like a desert flower that blooms against all odds, these devoted souls find their sustenance not from external praise but from a deeper, internal wellspring of fulfillment. In the quiet moments, the shared smiles, and the knowledge that they have comforted the suffering, they find their oasis of satisfaction.

Biblical References:

Drawing from the wellsprings of ancient wisdom, the Bible holds stories that resonate with the thankless nature of noble endeavors. In the Book of Matthew (6:1-4), Jesus emphasizes the importance of doing good deeds not for public recognition but for the inherent value of helping others. "Be careful not to practice your righteousness in front of others to be seen by them... But when you give to the needy, do not let your left hand know what your right hand is doing, so that your giving may be in secret."

In her journey, Antoinette Greendige embodies the tireless commitment of those who traverse this complex path. Through her eyes, the challenges of a profession often overlooked become evident—the emotional toll of bearing witness to human struggles, the unceasing battle to maintain professionalism in the face of anguish, and the perseverance required to provide unwavering care.

The Triumph of Compassion Over Recognition:

Antoinette Greendige's journey encapsulates the paradoxical coexistence of the thankless and fulfilling nature of the medical field. She is a testament to the triumph of compassion over recognition, of the internal rewards that fuel the dedication of healthcare professionals worldwide. For every patient whose pain she alleviated, for every family whose burden she lightened, she found herself replenished in ways that transcended the external clamor for praise.

Like the biblical Good Samaritan, her journey reflects the notion that true goodness and compassion are often quiet, humble acts. In Luke (10:33-35), the Samaritan tends to an injured man left by the wayside, nursing his wounds and providing for his care without seeking public acknowledgment. "But a Samaritan, as he traveled, came where the man was; and when he saw him, he took pity on him. He went to him and bandaged his wounds, pouring on oil and wine."

Bearing Witness to Humanity's Struggles:

In the medical field's labyrinth, healthcare professionals like Antoinette Greendige, bear witness to the myriad struggles that define the human condition. The emotionally charged encounters with patients and their families underscore the profundity of their calling. The bedside moments, the shared stories, and the often unspoken connections testify to the human capacity for empathy and healing.

As the apostle Paul exhorted in Romans (12:15), "Rejoice with those who rejoice; mourn with those who mourn." The medical field demands this emotional investment, this willingness to share in the joys and sorrows of others without seeking immediate recognition for one's efforts. Greendige's journey embodies this principle, standing as a living example of a soul dedicated to alleviating suffering, whether acknowledged by the world or not.

Bridging the Chasm: Professionalism Amidst Anguish:

Navigating the chasm between personal emotions and professional obligations is a hallmark of the medical field. Antoinette Greendige's journey exemplifies the delicate dance that healthcare professionals perform, upholding their commitment to healing while battling the anguish that often accompanies their patients' struggles. It is a journey of maintaining an unwavering demeanor while emotionally investing in the well-being of those under their care.

In the Gospel of Mark (1:40-42), the story of Jesus healing a leper captures this delicate balance: "A man with leprosy came to him and begged Him on his knees, 'If you are willing, you can make me clean.' Filled with compassion, Jesus reached out His hand and touched the man. 'I am willing,' he said. 'Be clean!'" Here, Jesus exemplifies professionalism and compassion, bridging the gap between His divine role and His humanity.

The Power of Perseverance:

The medical field's challenges demand perseverance of a unique kind. Antoinette Greendige's dedication to providing unwavering care, even in the face of exhaustion and personal sacrifices, mirrors the resilience demanded of healthcare professionals. Despite the lack of external recognition, the unrelenting pursuit of healing is a testament to their strength.

The Bible offers countless stories of perseverance, from Noah's dedication in building the ark to endure the flood (Genesis 6-9) to Job's unwavering faith amidst trials (Job 1-42). These narratives reflect the value of persisting in the face of challenges, a quality that resonates in the stories of healthcare professionals like Greendige, who persevere for the greater good.

In the Footsteps of the Divine Healer:

Ultimately, the journey of healthcare professionals like Antoinette Greendige echoes the footsteps of the Divine Healer himself. In the Gospels, Jesus is depicted as a compassionate and selfless healer who mends broken bodies and spirits alike. His ministry often took place away from the spotlight as he healed the sick, comforted the afflicted, and extended grace to the marginalized.

Matthew, in 9:35-36, writes, "Jesus went through all the towns and villages, teaching in their synagogues, proclaiming the good news of the kingdom and healing every disease and sickness. When he saw the crowds, he had compassion on them because they were harassed and helpless, like sheep without a shepherd." This empathy, this ability to see beyond the surface and into the depths of human suffering, encapsulates the essence of the medical field's journey.

A Path of Redemption:

Antoinette Greendige's path, much like the biblical narratives, is one of redemption. Her commitment, unwavering compassion, and ability to find fulfillment beyond the bounds of external recognition mirror the stories of those who, throughout history, have chosen the challenging path of healing and selfless service.

In Romans (8:18), the apostle Paul writes, "I consider that our present sufferings are not worth comparing with the glory that will be revealed in us." This sentiment resonates in the medical field, where the challenges faced pale compared to the immense impact of healing and the intrinsic.

The Core Foundations and Principles of Working Hard: A Blueprint for Success and Legacy Building

In the intricate tapestry of personal and professional development, pursuing success is often guided by principles and foundations that form the bedrock of a strong work ethic. The journey of working hard transcends mere effort; it encompasses a deliberate and strategic approach to achieving goals, fostering resilience, and ultimately leaving a lasting legacy. This exploration delves into the core foundations and principles constituting a blueprint for success and legacy building—a roadmap for individuals seeking personal triumphs and a profound, enduring impact that echoes through generations.

At the heart of this blueprint lies the principle of discipline, the steadfast commitment to structured habits that amplify focus, time management, and consistent effort. Combined with goal setting, this discipline becomes a powerful force, providing direction and purpose to the diligent individual. As we navigate the realms of perseverance and self-motivation, we uncover the resilience needed to weather challenges and the intrinsic drive that fuels sustained effort, even without immediate external incentives.

Continuous learning emerges as a fundamental principle, emphasizing the importance of staying adaptable and competitive in an ever-evolving landscape. Responsibility and accountability become guiding lights, shaping individuals into reliable and trustworthy contributors to their fields. Focusing on quality over quantity ensures that the fruits of hard work stand as achievements and enduring legacies of excellence.

As we explore the ethical dimension, we recognize the significance of upholding principles of integrity in all endeavors. Trust, the cornerstone of professional relationships, is cultivated through ethical conduct, laying the foundation for a robust and enduring reputation.

Beyond personal success, we delve into the cosmic reciprocity that unfolds when one commits to these principles. In its intricate dance, the universe responds to disciplined effort with opportunities, creating a reciprocal relationship between hard work and favorable circumstances. Moreover, we contemplate the generational impact of embodying these principles, understanding that the legacy built through hard work extends far beyond individual achievements, shaping the destinies of those who follow.

In this exploration, we invite individuals to reflect on these foundational principles to glean insights that extend beyond immediate success and towards a legacy that resonates through time. The core foundations and principles of working hard serve not only as a guide for personal triumph but as a transformative force shaping the universe's response to dedicated, principled effort—a symphony in which every individual's hard work contributes not only to their success but to the echoing melody of a legacy that endures through the ages.

Discipline:
- Discipline is the bedrock of a strong work ethic. It involves cultivating habits that facilitate focus, time management, and consistent effort. The disciplined individual achieves short-term goals and builds a foundation for long-term success.

Goal Setting:
- Setting well-defined goals provides a sense of direction and purpose. Achieving milestones creates a positive feedback loop, reinforcing the connection between hard work and

success. This, in turn, contributes to a mindset that embraces challenges as opportunities for growth.

Time Management:
- Effective time management ensures that every moment contributes to meaningful progress. Prioritizing tasks, avoiding multitasking, and dedicating focused time to important activities maximize productivity. The efficient use of time becomes a hallmark of the industrious individual.

Perseverance:
- Perseverance is the tenacity to weather storms and overcome obstacles. The resilience to persist, in the face of adversity, builds character and sets the stage for long-term success. The ability to endure challenges becomes a testament to one's commitment to personal and professional growth.

Self-Motivation:
- Self-motivation is the internal drive that sustains momentum. It involves finding purpose and passion in the work at hand, ensuring that effort is not solely dependent on external factors. A self-motivated individual remains committed even in the absence of immediate rewards.

Continuous Learning:
- A commitment to lifelong learning is a key element of a strong work ethic. Embracing opportunities for skill development, staying abreast of industry trends, and seeking out new knowledge contribute to adaptability and a competitive edge. Continuous learning positions individuals as leaders in their fields.

Responsibility and Accountability:
- Taking responsibility for one's actions and being accountable for outcomes fosters trust and reliability. The ability to own mistakes, learn from them, and actively seek improvement is a hallmark of a responsible individual. Accountability is the foundation of a solid professional reputation.

Resilience:
- Resilience is the ability to bounce back from setbacks stronger than before. Cultivating a mindset that views challenges as opportunities for growth transforms failures into stepping stones toward success. Resilience ensures that each setback becomes a valuable lesson learned.

Focus on Quality:
- Prioritizing quality over quantity is a distinguishing feature of a strong work ethic. Diligence, attention to detail, and a

commitment to excellence set the standard for the work produced. Pursuing quality ensures that the individual's contributions stand the test of time.

Ethics and Integrity:
- Upholding ethical standards and maintaining integrity in all interactions are non-negotiable principles. Trust is the currency of professional relationships, and ethical behavior forms the backbone of a solid reputation. A commitment to ethical conduct is an investment in long-term success.

The Universe's Repayment and Legacy:

The universe has a way of repaying individuals who embody these principles. As one works hard, demonstrates discipline, and achieves success, the universe responds by aligning circumstances in their favor. Opportunities unfold, connections are made, and success begets success. The energy invested in hard work creates a positive ripple effect, influencing not only personal outcomes but also impacting the lives of others.

The legacy of hard work extends beyond immediate success—it becomes a gift to future generations. By embodying these principles, individuals create a blueprint for success that transcends their lifetime. The values instilled, examples set, and impact on others form a lasting legacy. Hard work becomes a generational investment, influencing the trajectory of family, community, and societal success.

In essence, the principles of working hard shape personal success and contribute to a legacy that echoes through time. The universe repays the diligent with opportunities, and the legacy built becomes a beacon, guiding future generations toward their paths of success and fulfillment. Hard work, rooted in these principles, becomes a transformative force that shapes not only individual destinies but the very fabric of the universe's response to dedicated, principled effort.

KIDS WILL BE KIDS

Two Worlds, One Family: Cultural Tapestries and Identity

Amidst the sprawling urban landscape, a family is a testament to the intertwined narratives of immigration, heritage, and growth. As second-generation immigrants hailing from Trinidad and Tobago, they found themselves at the crossroads of two distinct worlds. This juxtaposition brings the challenge of maintaining their roots while embracing the fast-paced urban lifestyle they now call home. Their children are raised as bridges between these cultural spheres, their identities shaped by the richness of their ancestry and the vibrancy of their present environment. Just as the biblical character Ruth found herself rooted in a foreign land yet fully committed to the heritage of her husband's family, this family's journey is a testament to the fusion of old and new, of heritage and adaptation.

A Mother's Calling: The Nurse's Midnight Vigil

In the heart of their family, the mother's journey unfolds as a testament to her unyielding commitment. As she pursues a nursing career, her path is paved with sleepless nights of studying, tireless shifts at the hospital, and a dedication that knows no bounds. Her role mirrors the biblical parable of the Good Samaritan (Luke 10:25-37), where compassion transcends boundaries. Like the Samaritan who extended care to a stranger in need, this mother's calling recognizes no confines and encompasses her family and the broader community she serves.

A Father's Sacrifice: Tenacity and Financial Stability

Parallel to the mother's dedication, the father's tireless efforts paint a portrait of unwavering determination. Striving for financial stability, he embraces a full-time job while juggling multiple side endeavors to provide for his family's needs. His journey mirrors the biblical principle of diligence and provision, akin to the words of Proverbs 6:6-8: "Go to the ant, you sluggard; consider its ways and be wise! It has no commander, overseer, or ruler, yet it stores its provisions in summer and gathers its food at harvest." His actions echo this wisdom as he tirelessly gathers resources to ensure a secure future for his loved ones.

Children Within, One Cherished Soul Beyond:
Extending Love and Guidance

Within the walls of their home, this family nurtures and guides their three children through the ebbs and flows of growth. Milestones and teachable moments punctuate this journey, offering both celebration and opportunities for guidance. The family understands the essence of Proverbs 22:6: "Train up a child in the way he should go: and when he is old, he will not depart from it." Their guiding hands are not limited to those within their household. They extend their love and guidance to a cherished child living beyond their walls, ensuring that their spiritual support and influence have no bounds.

Navigating Urban Waters:
Spiritual Anchors in an Urban Landscape

Amid the urban sprawl, the family faces unique challenges. Amidst the bustling streets and towering structures, they remain steadfast in ensuring their children are spiritually covered, grounded, and protected. Living in an urban environment often inundated with distractions, they draw parallels with the biblical tale of Daniel in Babylon. Just as Daniel navigated a foreign culture while holding fast to his faith, this family ensures that their children grow up with an unshakeable sense of purpose, guided by spiritual principles.

Balancing Parenthood and Marriage: A Unified Front

While juggling the demands of parenthood and careers, the couple understands the importance of unity within their marriage. Ephesians 5:25 serves as their guiding light: "Husbands, love your wives, just as Christ loved the church and gave himself up for her." Their bond exemplifies the strength that arises from communication, mutual understanding, and shared goals. As they navigate the challenges of raising children in a bustling environment, their unified front ensures they are always on the same page, a pillar of strength amidst the chaos.

Milestones and Teachable Moments: Celebrating Growth

As the children progress through various stages of growth, the family embraces the universal truth that children will be children. From the innocent wonder of first steps to the tumultuous waters of adolescence, each milestone brings its own emotions and challenges. Likewise, stewards, these parents use each moment as an opportunity for growth. Just as the biblical account of the prodigal son demonstrates the power of return and redemption, these parents stand ready to guide their children through life's joys and trials.

The Unwavering Faith: Anchoring Amidst Storms

Amidst their journey's twists and turns, this family finds their faith to be an unwavering anchor. Proverbs 3:5-6 resonates deeply: "Trust in the Lord with all your heart and lean not on your own understanding; in all your ways submit to him, and he will make your paths straight." As Abraham embarked on a faith journey to an unknown land, this family navigates life's uncertainties with a profound trust in a higher purpose. Just as the biblical narrative showcases the rewards of unwavering faith, their story is a testament to the power of trust and resilience.

A Symphony of Love and Resilience:

In the harmonious symphony of challenges and blessings, this family's narrative is a testament to the power of unity, faith, and unyielding determination. Their journey reflects the profound love that guides them, the cultural heritage that shapes them, and the spiritual foundation that sustains them amidst the bustling urban tapestry of life. As they nurture their children, extend their love beyond their walls, and weather the storms and sunshine of life, their story echoes the profound truth that family is a sanctuary of love and a testament to the journey of the human spirit.

A FAITHFUL SERVANT

Being a faithful servant encompasses a deeply rooted commitment to serving a higher purpose, often guided by one's spiritual beliefs, values, and a sense of responsibility to others. It involves a profound dedication to the greater good, extending beyond personal interests and ego-driven desires. A faithful servant embodies humility, compassion, selflessness, and a genuine desire to contribute positively to the lives of others and the world at large.

Key Traits of a Faithful Servant:

- Humility: A faithful servant approaches their role humbly, recognizing that their actions are part of a larger tapestry. They acknowledge their strengths and limitations, never seeking personal recognition but rather focusing on the impact they can make.

- Compassion: Compassion lies at the heart of being a faithful servant. They genuinely care about the well-being and struggles of others, offering support, empathy, and kindness. Their actions are motivated by a sincere desire to alleviate suffering and uplift those around them.

- Selflessness: A faithful servant places the needs of others before their own. They willingly sacrifice personal comfort and desires to ensure the betterment of others. Their sense of fulfillment comes from their positive impact rather than seeking personal gain.

- Dedication: Being a faithful servant involves steadfast dedication to the cause or purpose they serve. They show up consistently, even when faced with challenges or obstacles, driven by an unwavering commitment to their responsibilities.

- Integrity: Integrity is a core value for a faithful servant. They uphold ethical principles and maintain honesty in their interactions. Their actions are guided by a solid moral compass that reflects their genuine intentions.

- Empowerment: A faithful servant seeks to empower others rather than exert control. They aim to uplift, encourage, and support those they serve, fostering an environment of growth and empowerment.

- Gratitude: Gratitude is an integral part of being a faithful servant. They recognize the privilege of being able to serve and are appreciative of the opportunities to make a positive impact.

Serving a Higher Purpose:

Being a faithful servant often involves aligning one's actions with a higher purpose rooted in religious beliefs, spiritual principles, or a deep sense of responsibility to humanity. This higher purpose gives their service a profound sense of meaning and fulfillment, transcending individual goals and contributing to the greater good.

Transcending Boundaries:

A faithful servant's service knows no boundaries. They extend their support and care beyond their immediate circle, reaching out to diverse communities, individuals, and causes. Their service is inclusive, recognizing the interconnectedness of all beings and the responsibility to create a better world for everyone.

Being a faithful servant goes beyond performing tasks or duties; it embodies a way of life characterized by humility, compassion, selflessness, and dedication to a higher purpose. It's about using one's abilities, resources, and time to positively impact the lives of others and the world as a whole. Through their actions, a faithful servant uplifts, empowers, and contributes to the well-being of individuals and society, leaving behind a legacy of service and compassion.

Antoinette Greendige:
A Portrait of a Faithful Servant Leader

In the tapestry of human existence, some stand as shining examples of what it truly means to be a servant leader. Antoinette Greendige was undoubtedly one of these exceptional souls, embodying the essence of selfless service, unwavering dedication, and a profound commitment to uplifting the lives of those around her. Throughout her remarkable journey, from the earliest days of her life to her final breath, Antoinette epitomized the very definition of a faithful servant leader.

A Life of Service and Sacrifice:

Antoinette's life was a testament to service, a symphony of selflessness that resonated through every facet of her existence. From her earliest memories, she understood that the true measure of a person's worth lay not in personal accomplishments but in their positive impact on others. This understanding propelled her to serve with a genuine heart, putting the needs of others before her own and willingly sacrificing her time, resources, and efforts to create a better world.

Community Caretaker:

In her local community, Antoinette's presence was a beacon of hope and kindness. Every Saturday, as the sun's first rays painted the sky, she diligently cleaned her church, a humble act of devotion that spoke volumes about her character. Cooking meals for community gatherings, family events, and work-related festivities was a labor of love for her. She nourished bodies and the spirit of unity and togetherness through her culinary talents.

Familial Pillar:

Antoinette's devotion to her family was unwavering and steadfast. She extended her love and support to her family financially and emotionally, becoming a cornerstone of stability during times of need. Her contributions were not just monetary; they were filled with a deep sense of caring and an understanding that family bonds are the foundation upon which lives are built.

Guiding Light of Spirituality:

As a minister, Antoinette's influence extended far beyond the confines of a church building. Her teachings resonated with people of all ages, from the youth seeking guidance to the adults looking for solace. Through her words, she nurtured faith, offered solace, and encouraged a life lived in service to others. Her spiritual guidance was not limited to the pulpit; it was woven into the fabric of her interactions, coloring every interaction with compassion and wisdom.

Mother and Wife:

Antoinette's love knew no bounds in the roles of mother and wife. Raising her children with a blend of nurturing and discipline, she instilled the values of empathy, integrity, and responsibility. As a wife, she exemplified the essence of partnership, supporting her husband through thick and thin, sharing the burdens of life, and celebrating its joys side by side.

A Lasting Legacy:

The sun dipped below the horizon, casting a warm orange glow across the serene landscape. The gentle rustling of leaves in the trees seemed to echo a quiet tribute to a life that had left an indelible mark on the world. Antoinette Greendige had departed from this earthly realm, but her legacy lived on, not in grand monuments or extravagant tributes, but in the hearts and lives of those she had touched.

Antoinette had never sought recognition or fame. Her journey had been of quiet determination, rooted in a deep understanding that leadership was not about wielding authority or amassing power but about selfless service to others. This fundamental principle had been woven into the very fabric of her being, shaping every decision she made and every action she took.

As news of Antoinette's passing spread, tributes poured in from all corners of the globe. World leaders, community members, colleagues, and friends all shared their stories of how Antoinette had touched their lives. However, it was clear that her legacy was not defined by the accolades she received or the material success she achieved; it was defined by her lasting impact on the people she served.

Antoinette's leadership style was a rare and precious gem. She led with a heart full of compassion, a mind guided by wisdom, and a spirit fueled by humility. Those who worked alongside her couldn't help but be inspired by her unwavering dedication to uplifting others. She believed true leadership meant rolling up one's sleeves and standing shoulder to shoulder with those in need, regardless of personal cost.

Her footsteps had left imprints on the paths she had walked, not of authority, but of empathy. She had shown that leadership was not a solitary journey but a collective endeavor that required fostering a sense of unity and purpose among those she led. Through her actions, she instilled a sense of belonging and camaraderie that transcended hierarchy and titles.

In the days following her passing, a memorial service was held in her honor. The gathering was not a somber affair but a celebration of a life well-lived. Stories were shared, laughter echoed through the air, and tears flowed freely, each tear a testament to the profound impact she had left behind.

As the sun set on the day of the memorial, a hush fell over the assembled crowd. It was a moment of reflection, a moment to ponder the legacy that Antoinette had left for them to carry forward. Her life had been a tapestry woven with threads of love, compassion, and inspiration. It was a tapestry that would continue to unfold in the lives of those she had influenced.

Antoinette's legacy was a guiding light, a beacon that reminded them all that leadership was not measured in titles or wealth but in the lives they touched and the hearts they uplifted. Her story was a reminder that the impact of a life lived in service extended far beyond its earthly years. It was a reminder that a single individual, armed with nothing but a heart full of kindness and a commitment to serving others, could change the world.

In the annals of history, Antoinette Greendige's name will forever be synonymous with the spirit of a faithful servant leader. Her life illuminated the path of selfless service, which required sacrifice and humility. Her legacy was not confined to the pages of a history book; it was alive in the actions of those who had learned from her example.

As the sun dipped below the horizon and the stars began to twinkle in the night sky, those who had gathered to honor Antoinette felt a renewed sense of purpose. They knew that her legacy was not just a memory but a living, breathing force that would continue to shape their actions, decisions, and interactions with the world around them.

And so, Antoinette's legacy lived on, not in grand monuments of stone, but in the hearts and lives of those she had touched. The story of her life would be passed down through generations, a story of compassion, humility, and unwavering dedication to the well-being of others. Her legacy would continue to inspire, remind, and guide, ensuring that the world would forever be a better place because of her presence.

**Everyday Counts:
Embracing the Gift of Limited Time**

In the poignant shadow of a diagnosis, life undergoes a profound transformation, taking on new hues that reflect the stark reality of life's impermanence. This chapter invites a deep exploration into the journey of embracing the gift of limited time—an odyssey that extends beyond mere existence to one of intentional living, profound introspection, and the nurturing of meaningful connections with family, self, and the Divine. As the grains of sand steadily flow through the hourglass, each moment becomes a precious gem, and individuals are encouraged to weave these gems into a tapestry of purpose, significance, and enduring memories.

Facing the Reality:

A diagnosis serves as a crossroads, a juncture demanding reflection and the reassessment of life's priorities. In the face of such news, the trivialities that once occupied our attention gradually fade into the background, making room for a more profound contemplation of our life's journey. Emotions ranging from fear and uncertainty to, perhaps even anger surface, creating a whirlwind of turmoil. Yet, amid this emotional tempest, a seed of transformation is planted—an opportunity for growth, a chance to reorient our perspectives, and an invitation to align our lives with what truly matters.

Living with Intention:

With the awareness of limited time, living with intentionality transforms from a mere choice into an imperative. The automated routines that once filled our days are reconsidered, and we consciously mold our moments with purpose. Every action and every decision becomes a brushstroke on the canvas of our existence, contributing to the masterpiece of our life's legacy. The question shifts from the mundane, "What do I have to do today?" to the profound, "How can I make today count?"

Cherishing Family Connections:

Often the cornerstone of our emotional landscape, the family assumes an even more significant role in this intentional journey. Realizing that time with loved ones is a treasure to be nurtured, celebrated, and savored becomes acutely apparent. Gatherings around tables are laden with food, stories, laughter, and shared experiences. Fences are mended, bonds are deepened, and efforts are made to ensure that love and memories remain a tapestry of unity even after we are no longer physically present.

Cultivating Self-Care:

Once considered an occasional indulgence, self-care transforms into profound self-love and preservation. Acknowledging that our bodies are vessels guiding us through life's journey, a conscious effort is made to prioritize well-being in all physical, emotional, and spiritual dimensions. Engaging in activities that bring joy, practicing mindfulness, prioritizing rest, and embracing healthy habits become not merely tasks but profound expressions of gratitude for the vessel that houses our spirit.

Deepening Spiritual Connection:

The journey of intentionality extends to our relationship with the Divine. As mortality's specter looms, our connection with the spiritual realm assumes heightened significance. Practices such as prayer, meditation, reflection, and seeking higher guidance become not only solace but vital tools as we navigate the uncharted territories of our existence. This connection serves as a wellspring of strength, a reminder that while our time on Earth is fleeting, our souls are woven into an eternal tapestry.

Leaving a Lasting Legacy:

In this journey of intentional living, the understanding emerges that the legacy we leave is not measured merely in the number of years we lived but in the impact we had on the lives of others. Contemplating the mark we want to leave on the world becomes a profound exercise—a legacy reflecting our values, passions, and the essence of our being. Through acts of kindness, creative endeavors, and inspiring moments, we weave a legacy that resonates with the hearts of those who will carry our memory forward.

Embracing Every Day:

In the grand symphony of life, every day is a note, and every note contributes to the melody of our existence. Guided by the specter of limited time, we embark on a journey that celebrates the beauty of each sunrise and the grace of each sunset. We dance in the rain, linger in the embrace of loved ones, and immerse ourselves in the presence of the Divine. Every moment becomes a canvas, painted with the hues of our intentions and the love that permeates our existence.

While the diagnosis may be an unwelcome guest, it catalyzes a journey of unparalleled depth and meaning. The awareness that our days are numbered propels us toward a life lived with intentionality, purpose, and profound introspection. Each day is embraced as a gift, and moments are woven together to form the rich tapestry of our legacy. This legacy transcends our earthly sojourn, leaving footprints of love, intention, and significance that will resonate through time. Even in the face of limited time, life becomes a masterpiece of purpose and profound connection, reminding us that every day counts.

HOW DID THEY MISS IT?

As adults, the conscientious endeavor to proactively maintain good health is a cornerstone for leading a fulfilling and vibrant life. This commitment involves a holistic approach that transcends the routine of daily habits, extending into the realm of regular health check-ups and annual lab tests. These examinations are critical elements of preventive healthcare, allowing individuals to detect and address potential health issues at their nascent stages. By adopting such proactive measures, individuals empower themselves with a deeper understanding of their overall well-being and lay the groundwork for minimizing the risk of diseases that could otherwise impact their quality of life.

Regular check-ups hold significant value in preventive healthcare as they allow healthcare professionals to assess various aspects of an individual's health. These assessments include monitoring vital signs, evaluating organ function, and conducting screenings for common health concerns. Early detection of issues such as high blood pressure, elevated cholesterol levels, or irregular blood sugar can lead to timely interventions, preventing the progression of these conditions into more serious health challenges. Through regular check-ups, individuals forge partnerships with their healthcare providers, actively engaging in a collaborative effort to safeguard and optimize their health.

Annual lab tests complement routine check-ups by providing a more in-depth analysis of physiological markers and biomarkers. Blood tests, for example, can offer insights into cholesterol levels, blood glucose, and organ function. These tests serve as proactive tools for identifying potential risk factors for cardiovascular diseases, diabetes, and various other health conditions. The comprehensive data derived from lab tests empowers individuals to make informed decisions about their lifestyle, nutrition, and overall health management, contributing to a more personalized and preventive approach to well-being.

Beyond the physical health benefits, regular check-ups and lab tests are a testament to individuals' proactive stance in prioritizing their health. It reflects a commitment to self-care and a recognition of the profound impact that preventive measures can have on long-term health outcomes. By incorporating these practices into their lives, individuals gain a deeper understanding of their health status and cultivate a sense of responsibility for their well-being. This commitment sets the stage for a life characterized by vitality, resilience, and the pursuit of lasting health and happiness. In essence, regular check-ups and lab tests become integral components of a holistic approach to well-being, marking the proactive steps adults can take to nurture their health and enrich their lives.

1. Annual Physical Examination:

An annual physical exam is a cornerstone of preventive healthcare. During this visit, your healthcare provider will review your medical history, assess your vital signs, and perform a comprehensive physical examination. This examination helps identify potential health concerns, monitor existing conditions, and ensure your general health is on track.

2. Blood Pressure Check:

High blood pressure (hypertension) is often referred to as the "silent killer" because it may not have noticeable symptoms. Regular blood pressure checks can help detect hypertension early, reducing the risk of heart disease, stroke, and kidney problems.

3. Cholesterol Levels:

An annual cholesterol screening measures your LDL (bad) cholesterol, HDL (good) cholesterol, and total cholesterol levels. Abnormal cholesterol levels can contribute to heart disease. Early detection allows for lifestyle changes and, if necessary, medical intervention to manage cholesterol levels.

4. Blood Glucose Test:

Regular blood glucose tests help monitor your blood sugar levels and detect diabetes or prediabetes early. Early intervention and lifestyle changes can prevent complications associated with diabetes.

5. Cancer Screenings:

Cancer screenings are vital for early detection, as treatment outcomes are often better when cancer is identified in its early stages. Standard cancer screenings include:

- Mammogram: Recommended for women to detect breast cancer.
- Pap Smear: Recommended for women to screen for cervical cancer.

- Colonoscopy: Recommended for both men and women to screen for colorectal cancer.
- Prostate-Specific Antigen (PSA) Test: Recommended for men to screen for prostate cancer.

6. Immunizations:

Keeping up-to-date with recommended vaccinations is an important aspect of preventive healthcare. Vaccines protect against various diseases and help build immunity. Consult your healthcare provider to ensure your immunization schedule is current.

7. Bone Density Test:

A bone density test measures bone strength and can identify osteoporosis, a condition that weakens bones and makes them more prone to fractures. Early detection allows for lifestyle changes and treatment to prevent fractures.

8. Skin Check:

An annual skin check by a dermatologist helps detect skin cancer early. Early diagnosis of skin cancer improves treatment outcomes and reduces the risk of complications.

9. Eye Exam:

Regular eye exams help monitor your vision and eye health. Eye conditions such as glaucoma and age-related macular degeneration can be detected and managed early, preserving your vision.

10. Dental Check-Up:

Routine dental visits for cleanings and check-ups help maintain oral health. Good oral hygiene is linked to overall health, and early detection of dental issues prevents complications.

Proactive healthcare involves a partnership between you and your healthcare provider. By following the recommended routine visits and annual lab tests, you empower yourself with the knowledge to make informed health decisions. Early detection and prevention are valuable keys to leading a healthy and fulfilling life, minimizing the risk of diseases, and maximizing your well-being. Always consult your healthcare provider to tailor these recommendations to your health needs.

Balancing LPN Expertise with Spiritual Strength

Antoinette's life journey was a testament to her commitment to health, rooted in her medical expertise as an LPN and her unwavering faith as a spiritual intercessor. With a unique blend of medical knowledge and a deep connection to her Trinidadian roots, she embraced conventional and natural remedies while remaining spiritually resilient in the face of challenges.

A Holistic Approach to Health:

Antoinette's dual perspective as an LPN and a believer in natural remedies allowed her to embrace a holistic approach to health. She understood the importance of seeking medical advice while acknowledging the potential benefits of natural remedies. Her Trinidadian heritage instilled in her a deep appreciation for the healing properties of herbs and natural substances, and she incorporated these remedies into her health regimen. Through this balanced approach, she showcased her commitment to staying informed and proactive about her well-being.

Navigating the Challenges:

As the years passed, Antoinette encountered the aches and pains that can accompany a life of hard work and spiritual service. Her role as a medical professional exposed her to physical demands, while her dedication as a prayer warrior and intercessor placed her amid spiritual battles. These challenges tested not only her physical resilience but also her spiritual strength.

The Role of an Intercessor:

An intercessor is a spiritual warrior who stands in the gap between individuals and the divine, offering prayers and supplications on behalf of others. This role requires a deep connection to one's spirituality and a willingness to intercede for the needs and concerns of others. An intercessor acts as a bridge, channeling divine intervention and comfort to those in need.

Spiritual Resilience:

Antoinette's life as an intercessor demanded an unshakable spiritual foundation. The Bible speaks of spiritual warfare, where believers are encouraged to "Put on the full armor of God so that you can take your stand against the devil's schemes" (Ephesians 6:11, NIV). This armor includes truth, righteousness, faith, salvation, and the Word of God. Through this spiritual armor, intercessors stand strong against spiritual attacks, offering prayers as a shield of protection.

Biblical References:

Antoinette drew strength from various biblical references that fortified her spiritual resilience. The words of Isaiah 41:10 became a source of comfort: "So do not fear, for I am with you; do not be dismayed, for I am your God. I will strengthen you and help you; I will uphold you with my righteous right hand" (NIV). This promise of God's presence and support provided solace during moments of fatigue and spiritual battles.

The Unanswered Questions

Antoinette's journey was a testament to her dedication to health as a medical professional and a believer in holistic well-being. Yet, her narrative took a somber turn as she encountered a baffling challenge within the healthcare system to which she had devoted her life. Despite her adherence to medical protocols, repeated visits to the doctor, and a cascade of concerning symptoms, her diagnosis remained elusive. How could the healthcare system she had trusted and served fail to recognize her plight? This tale raises questions about the complexities of medical practice, the challenges of diagnosis, and the human dimension of healthcare.

Advanced Technology and Missed Clues:

In an era of advanced medical technology, it is perplexing to consider how Antoinette's diagnosis could be missed. With a plethora of diagnostic tools at their disposal, from sophisticated imaging to comprehensive lab tests, healthcare professionals are equipped to uncover even the most subtle anomalies. Antoinette's recurrent falls, breathing difficulties, and ongoing health concerns should have prompted thorough investigations, yielding a comprehensive diagnosis. How could her symptoms go unnoticed despite the available resources?

The Burden of Being a Healthcare Professional:

Antoinette's unique position as a medical professional should have theoretically provided her with an advantage. Her knowledge of healthcare intricacies and familiarity with the importance of thorough evaluations should have ensured that her concerns were taken seriously. However, the reality can be more complex. Being a healthcare professional herself might have inadvertently influenced how her colleagues perceived her complaints. Often, assumptions can arise that a fellow healthcare worker is more knowledgeable about their health or their symptoms might be less serious.

Communication and Patient Advocacy:

Communication is a cornerstone of effective healthcare. Patients should feel heard, validated, and empowered to advocate for their well-being. In Antoinette's case, her reoccurring issues and pleas for answers seemed to be dismissed. This raises questions about the importance of patient advocacy and the necessity of a healthcare system that values patients' voices and concerns. Were her requests for further investigations met with skepticism, leading to a delay in diagnosis?

The Complexity of Diagnosis:

Medicine is an intricate blend of science and art, where diagnosis often involves deciphering a mosaic of symptoms, medical history, and test results. Sometimes, symptoms can be deceptive, mimicking multiple conditions or defying straightforward categorization. Even with advanced technology, misdiagnoses and missed diagnoses can occur due to the complexity of the human body and the unpredictability of certain conditions.

The Quest for Answers:

Antoinette's journey underscores the critical importance of a healthcare system that places patients at the center. It reminds us that no individual, regardless of their medical background, is immune to the challenges of medical practice. The missed diagnosis raises awareness about the need for healthcare professionals to listen intently, communicate effectively, and continuously explore all avenues to uncover the underlying causes of symptoms.

Antoinette's experience within the healthcare system serves as a poignant reminder that while medical science has advanced leaps and bounds, the human element of healthcare remains paramount. Her story challenges us to reevaluate how we engage with patients, emphasizing the value of open communication, patient advocacy, and a thorough exploration of symptoms. As we seek to understand the complexities of her journey, we are prompted to consider how the convergence of technology, human perception, and the pursuit of answers intertwine to shape the healthcare landscape for professionals and patients alike.

Be Yourself

Know Yourself: Be your advocate invites individuals to embark on a profound journey within the intricate symphony of life, where the human body is a remarkable vessel—a marvel of biological intricacy. This journey unfolds as a tapestry woven from threads of science, intuition, and self-awareness. It is a narrative that extends beyond mere existence, calling for an active engagement in understanding and caring for this complex creation; from deciphering subtle signals to navigating when to seek professional medical advice and even embracing holistic approaches, the path to optimal health beckons for a harmonious blend of knowledge and mindfulness.

In this intricate symphony, recognizing the subtle signals the body communicates becomes a foundational step. Every twinge, fluctuation in energy, or emotional nuance forms a part of this language. Being attuned to these signals fosters heightened self-awareness, allowing individuals to decode their bodies' intricate messages. This self-awareness, rooted in the art of listening to one's body, becomes a powerful tool for proactive health management.

The role of being one's advocate extends beyond self-awareness to navigating when to seek professional medical advice. While self-awareness provides valuable insights, there are instances where the expertise of medical professionals is indispensable. Understanding the balance between recognizing personal signals and seeking professional guidance creates a synergy that contributes to a comprehensive approach to health. Regular check-ups, screenings, and consultations become proactive steps in advocating for one's well-being.

Embracing holistic approaches further enriches this journey of self-advocacy. It involves recognizing that optimal health extends beyond the physical realm to encompass mental, emotional, and spiritual well-being. Practices such as mindfulness, nutrition, and alternative therapies are integral to this holistic approach. By actively engaging in these practices, individuals advocate for a more comprehensive understanding of health beyond the reductionist view of the body as a collection of separate parts.

Therefore, the path to optimal health is a harmonious blend of knowledge and mindfulness. It is a journey where individuals actively participate in their well-being, leveraging scientific understanding and intuitive wisdom. Being one's advocate involves making informed choices based on a deep connection with oneself and actively contributing to decisions that align with personal values, preferences, and holistic well-being.

Know Yourself: Be your advocate encapsulates a philosophy of empowerment and active engagement in pursuing optimal health. It is an invitation to explore the intricate symphony of the body, acknowledging the marvel of biological intricacy. Through a harmonious blend of science, intuition, and self-awareness, individuals can navigate the path to optimal health, advocating for their well-being with a sense of purpose and mindfulness. In this journey, the human body becomes a vessel and canvas painted with the strokes of self-discovery and holistic vitality.

The Art of Self-Awareness is a profound journey that delves into the intricate layers of our being, unraveling the wisdom embedded in the body's innate intelligence. Beyond the surface of our daily lives, the body constantly communicates with us through an intricate language of sensations and signals. Each heartbeat, breath, and even the subtlest twinge carry a message that is key to understanding our physical and mental well-being. This journey of self-discovery begins by tuning in and fostering a deep connection with the body's whispers.

One significant aspect of this art lies in paying attention to the nuances of our physical state. Changes in energy levels serve as a compass guiding us through the ebb and flow of life. For instance, feeling a surge of energy might indicate excitement or passion, while a sudden dip could signify the need for rest or self-care. Likewise, alterations in sleep patterns become clues to the body's needs and stresses. Recognizing the quality of sleep, the duration, and any disruptions provides valuable insights into overall health.

Digestion, often overlooked in the hustle of modern life, becomes a focal point in the art of self-awareness. Our bodies communicate their nutritional needs and sensitivities through the digestive process. Mindful eating and paying attention to how different foods make us feel can uncover hidden connections between diet and well-being. For instance, noticing discomfort after consuming certain foods may indicate intolerances or allergies, prompting adjustments for better health.

Mood, the intricate dance of emotions, is another canvas upon which self-awareness paints its strokes. By observing the ebb and flow of emotions, individuals gain a deeper understanding of their mental landscape. Awareness of mood fluctuations allows for identifying stressors, triggers, and patterns. This insight becomes a powerful tool for cultivating emotional resilience and fostering a more balanced inner state.

The practice of mindfulness becomes a cornerstone in this journey of self-awareness. Mindfulness involves being present in the moment and fully engaged with one's thoughts, feelings, and sensations. Through meditation and mindful living, individuals develop the capacity to observe the mind without judgment, creating a space for self-reflection and understanding. This heightened awareness extends beyond the physical and mental realms, encompassing the interconnectedness of body, mind, and spirit.

The art of self-awareness is not confined to moments of stillness; it extends into the activities of daily life. It involves conscious choices in moving, consuming, and interacting with the world. For example, a mindful walk in nature becomes an opportunity to connect with the environment, grounding oneself in the present moment. When approached with intention and awareness, even mundane tasks contribute to the ongoing masterpiece of self-discovery.

The body's language is not static; it evolves, responding to life's ever-changing landscape. Regular self-check-ins and moments of introspection become a ritual in this art. Taking time to reflect on the day and acknowledging challenges and triumphs fosters a continuous dialogue with the self. This reflective process cultivates a sense of agency and empowerment as individuals become active participants in their well-being.

Furthermore, the art of self-awareness extends its tendrils into interpersonal relationships. Understanding one's triggers, communication styles, and emotional responses enhances the quality of connections with others. It enables individuals to navigate relationships with empathy and authenticity, contributing to a harmonious social tapestry.

In essence, the art of self-awareness is a multifaceted masterpiece, a lifelong exploration of the self. It is a journey that involves tuning in to the body's messages, decoding the language of sensations, and embracing the ever-evolving nature of being. Individuals embark on a transformative path toward holistic well-being through mindfulness, conscious choices, and introspection. On this path, the canvas of the self is painted with vibrant hues of self-discovery and understanding.

Listening to the whispers of the body is an art that requires attunement to the subtle signals and messages it conveys. These whispers, often gentle and easily overlooked, serve as early indicators of the body's needs and concerns well before manifesting as urgent shouts of distress. Understanding and responding to these whispers form the foundation of proactive and preventative health care.

One of the primary aspects of this art involves recognizing changes in energy levels. A sudden dip in energy can be an early sign of impending illness or fatigue. By paying attention to these whispers, individuals can take preemptive measures such as adjusting their sleep patterns, incorporating restorative practices, or making necessary lifestyle changes. In doing so, they actively engage in self-care, preventing the escalation of potential health issues.

Often dismissed as commonplace, headaches are another form of communication from the body. Persistent headaches may indicate dehydration, stress, or other underlying issues. Rather than reaching for a pain reliever to silence the symptom, listening to the whisper prompts a deeper inquiry into the root cause. Adequate hydration, stress management techniques, or addressing any underlying health concerns can become part of the holistic approach to well-being.

The body's whispers extend beyond physical sensations to encompass emotional and mental states. For instance, heightened stress levels may manifest as tension in the shoulders or tightness in the chest—a subtle whisper that calls for stress-reducing interventions. By acknowledging these physical manifestations of emotional states, individuals can employ strategies such as meditation, deep breathing, or seeking support to address the underlying causes of stress.

Furthermore, digestive whispers play a significant role in the body's communication. Discomfort, bloating, or irregularities in digestion can signify dietary sensitivities or imbalances. Listening to these digestive whispers involves mindful eating and noting how different foods impact the body. Adjusting dietary choices based on these subtle signals contributes to digestive well-being and overall health.

An open heart, metaphorically representing a receptive and non-judgmental mindset, is crucial in deciphering these whispers. The art of listening to the body requires an attunement that goes beyond the analytical mind—it involves cultivating an intuitive connection with one's own physical and emotional landscape. This open-hearted approach allows individuals to receive and interpret the messages with clarity and understanding.

In the context of the art of listening to the whispers, preventative health practices become a natural outcome. Regular health check-ins, self-assessments, and reflective moments contribute to an ongoing dialogue with the body. This proactive engagement enables individuals to make informed decisions about their health, addressing concerns before they reach a critical stage.

Moreover, the art of listening to the whispers extends beyond the individual realm to interpersonal dynamics. A person attuned to their needs and whispers will likely be more empathetic and understanding in their relationships. Recognizing and respecting the subtle cues from others is integral to building meaningful connections.

The art of listening to the whispers is a nuanced and intricate journey of self-awareness and proactive health management. It involves deciphering the body's subtle messages, acknowledging energy changes, understanding the language of headaches, and tuning into emotional and digestive whispers. An open heart, combined with a commitment to preventative health practices, transforms listening into a powerful tool for overall well-being. This tool allows individuals to respond to the body's whispers with wisdom and care.

Knowing when to seek professional guidance is integral to navigating the complexities of health and well-being. While self-awareness is a powerful tool, understanding its limitations is paramount. In the realm of health, humility becomes a guiding principle, acknowledging that there are instances where personal knowledge may fall short, and the expertise of medical professionals is indispensable.

One key facet of this awareness is recognizing the gravity of persistent or severe symptoms. While individuals can interpret their body's signals to a certain extent, there are moments when symptoms may indicate underlying conditions that require professional evaluation. Understanding the threshold between normal fluctuations and potential health concerns is a crucial skill in the art of self-awareness.

Unexplained pain, a mysterious and often disconcerting whisper from the body, is a clear signal for seeking professional guidance. Rather than attempting to self-diagnose, it is wise to consult medical professionals with the expertise to conduct thorough assessments. The complexity of pain requires a nuanced understanding, and healthcare professionals can provide accurate diagnoses and recommend appropriate interventions.

Sudden changes in health status, whether manifested as a shift in energy levels, unexplained weight loss, or alterations in cognitive function, should prompt a proactive response. These abrupt changes may signify underlying health issues that demand prompt attention. Medical professionals with scientific knowledge and diagnostic tools are best positioned to unravel the intricacies of such changes and formulate tailored treatment plans.

The humility to recognize when professional guidance is necessary extends beyond acknowledging symptoms. It encompasses an understanding that healthcare is a collaborative effort between individuals and their medical providers. Routine check-ups, preventive screenings, and consultations with healthcare professionals contribute to proactive health management, ensuring early detection and intervention.

In the journey of knowing when to seek professional guidance, the role of healthcare professionals is pivotal. Their specialized knowledge, honed through rigorous education and practical experience, enables them to navigate the human body's complexities. Beyond diagnosis, they serve as educators, providing information and guidance to empower individuals to make informed health decisions.

Furthermore, professional guidance goes beyond physical health, encompassing mental and emotional well-being. Mental health professionals, such as psychologists and therapists, play a crucial role in addressing the complexities of the mind. Seeking their guidance is a proactive step in managing stress, anxiety, and other mental health challenges that may impact overall well-being.

In summary, while self-awareness is a valuable tool, it is complemented by the humility to recognize the boundaries of personal knowledge. Knowing when to seek professional guidance is an essential skill in the pursuit of optimal health. The art lies in discerning when symptoms surpass the realm of self-management and require the expertise of medical professionals. This collaborative approach of combining self-awareness with professional guidance forms the foundation of a comprehensive and proactive approach to health and well-being.

The synergy of medical and holistic approaches represents a paradigm shift, transcending the perceived division between conventional medicine and holistic practices. Rather than viewing them as opposing forces, this approach envisions a harmonious synergy that amplifies the potential for holistic well-being. Conventional medicine excels in addressing acute conditions, emergencies, and situations requiring precise intervention, while holistic practices delve into the interconnectedness of mind, body, and spirit. By seamlessly integrating the strengths of both, individuals can access a comprehensive care model that attends to the intricacies of both physical and emotional aspects of health.

Conventional medicine's prowess in managing acute conditions and emergencies is undeniable. It provides swift and targeted solutions to pressing health issues, from surgical interventions to pharmaceutical treatments. In situations demanding immediate and precise action, the expertise of medical professionals in conventional medicine is invaluable. The synergy emerges when this acute care is complemented by the holistic perspective, creating a more nuanced and thorough approach to well-being.

Holistic practices, on the other hand, recognize the importance of considering the whole person—mind, body, and spirit. Approaches such as acupuncture, yoga, meditation, and dietary modifications address the symptoms and underlying imbalances contributing to health issues. Holistic practitioners often emphasize preventive measures and lifestyle modifications, viewing health as a dynamic equilibrium that requires continuous attention. This perspective enriches the overall care experience by acknowledging the interconnected nature of various aspects of well-being.

Integrating these two approaches cultivates a more patient-centered and comprehensive healthcare model. For instance, a patient recovering from surgery may benefit from the precision of medical interventions and holistic practices that support mental and emotional healing. Mindfulness techniques, therapeutic exercises, and nutritional guidance can enhance recovery and contribute to a more holistic rehabilitation process.

Moreover, the synergy of medical and holistic approaches encourages a proactive stance towards health. Preventive screenings, routine check-ups, and early interventions from the medical perspective are seamlessly complemented by holistic practices that focus on maintaining balance and preventing imbalances from escalating into acute conditions. This collaboration between conventional medicine's acute care and holistic practices' preventative ethos forms a robust foundation for overall well-being.

The holistic approach also extends its influence into the realm of chronic conditions. While conventional medicine manages symptoms and provides necessary medications, holistic practices contribute by addressing lifestyle factors, stress management, and emotional well-being. This collaborative effort aims to treat the condition and improve the quality of life for individuals with chronic health challenges.

The synergy of medical and holistic approaches represents a transformative model in healthcare. It bridges the gap between acute interventions and holistic well-being, acknowledging the strengths of each approach. This integration fosters a more patient-centered, comprehensive, and proactive approach to health—a model that embraces the complexity of human well-being by recognizing the interconnected nature of the mind, body, and spirit.

Balancing Choice and Expertise is a delicate dance in seeking professional advice for health and well-being. It necessitates an open mind and a discerning heart, fostering a collaborative relationship with medical practitioners that empowers individuals to make informed decisions about their health. From diagnostic tests to prescribed medications, understanding the rationale behind medical interventions becomes a cornerstone for building trust in the process.

Approaching professional advice with an open mind involves acknowledging the expertise of medical practitioners while actively participating in the decision-making process. Effective communication between individuals and healthcare providers forms the basis of this collaboration. By asking questions, seeking clarification, and expressing concerns, individuals become partners in their care, ensuring a shared understanding of the proposed interventions.

Discernment plays a pivotal role in this balancing act. It involves critically evaluating the information provided by healthcare professionals, considering individual preferences, and weighing the potential benefits and risks of proposed treatments. This discerning approach allows individuals to make choices that align with their values, lifestyle, and overall health goals. It also encourages a sense of agency and autonomy in the decision-making process.

Understanding the rationale behind medical interventions is a crucial element in fostering trust. Armed with years of education and experience, medical practitioners can provide insights into the necessity and potential outcomes of various treatments. Transparent communication about the expected benefits, possible side effects, and alternative options empowers individuals to make decisions that resonate with their unique circumstances.

In the journey of balancing choice and expertise, seeking a second opinion emerges as a valid and prudent choice. It is not a challenge to the authority of the initial medical advice but rather a proactive step toward a more comprehensive understanding of the available treatment options. A second opinion provides a fresh perspective, allowing individuals to consider alternative approaches and ensuring a well-rounded view of their health situation.

Moreover, collaboration with medical practitioners extends beyond specific treatments to encompass broader aspects of health and well-being. Lifestyle modifications, preventive measures, and holistic approaches may be integral to the overall care plan. Engaging in open dialogue about these aspects allows individuals to actively participate in shaping a comprehensive approach to their health.

The balancing act between choice and expertise becomes particularly crucial when multiple treatment options exist or when facing complex medical decisions. In these instances, the collaborative relationship with healthcare providers becomes a dynamic exchange of information, preferences, and expertise to achieve the best possible outcome for the individual's health.

The journey of balancing choice and expertise in seeking professional advice is a nuanced and individualized process. It involves an open-minded approach, active collaboration with medical practitioners, discerning decision-making, and a commitment to understanding the rationale behind proposed interventions. Seeking a second opinion adds depth to this process, contributing to a more informed and empowered decision-making journey. This balanced approach enhances trust in the healthcare process and ensures that individuals actively contribute to shaping their path to well-being.

Exploring holistic approaches is a journey into a diverse realm of practices, each offering its unique philosophy and benefits to enhance overall well-being. Holistic practices acknowledge the interconnectedness of mind, body, and spirit, aiming to foster balance and harmony. Various techniques contribute to holistic wellness in this expansive landscape, inviting individuals to actively engage in their health journey.

Acupuncture, rooted in traditional Chinese medicine, is a holistic practice that taps into the body's energy meridians. By inserting thin needles into specific points, acupuncture aims to promote the flow of energy, or Qi, to restore balance. This ancient technique is renowned for addressing a myriad of physical and emotional imbalances, offering a holistic approach to health that considers the body as a dynamic and interconnected system.

Meditation, another integral, holistic practice, provides a pathway to cultivate mindfulness and reduce stress. Meditation encourages individuals to be present in the moment through focused attention and breath awareness, fostering mental clarity and emotional well-being. The holistic benefits extend beyond stress reduction, encompassing enhanced self-awareness, improved concentration, and a deeper connection to one's inner self.

Herbal remedies constitute a holistic approach that draws from nature's vast pharmacopeia. Plants and herbs offer a wealth of therapeutic compounds that can support the body's natural healing processes. From teas and tinctures to herbal supplements, this approach embraces the wisdom of traditional and alternative medicine, providing gentle and often sustainable methods to address various health concerns.

Nutritional therapies form a crucial component of holistic approaches, recognizing the profound impact of food on overall health. This approach goes beyond conventional nutrition, viewing food as sustenance and a powerful tool for nourishing and restoring the body. Holistic nutrition considers individual needs, dietary sensitivities, and the therapeutic properties of different foods, aiming to create a balanced and personalized approach to well-being.

Exploring these holistic approaches invites one to actively participate in one's well-being. Rather than viewing health as a passive experience, individuals engage in a proactive and empowering journey. This active participation involves learning about different holistic practices, experimenting with techniques that resonate, and incorporating them into daily life to create a comprehensive and sustainable approach to health.

The holistic approach is not a one-size-fits-all paradigm; it recognizes the uniqueness of each individual. Tailoring these practices to personal preferences and needs allows for a more meaningful and effective integration into one's lifestyle. Whether incorporating acupuncture sessions into a wellness routine, dedicating time to daily meditation, or exploring the benefits of herbal supplements, the journey of exploration is inherently personal and adaptable.

Exploring holistic approaches is an ongoing discovery, self-care, and empowerment process. It encourages individuals to actively participate in their well-being, embracing holistic wellness beyond alleviating symptoms to nurture the body, mind, and spirit. This holistic journey becomes a tapestry woven with the threads of ancient wisdom, nature's bounty, and the individual's conscious efforts to achieve and maintain a harmonious state of health.

Understanding the mind-body connection unveils the intricate and profound interconnection between the mind and body. This dynamic relationship signifies that the state of one significantly influences the other, underscoring the importance of recognizing and nurturing this symbiotic link. Emotional well-being, a facet of the mind, can directly impact physical health; conversely, the body's state influences our emotional state. Practices such as meditation, yoga, and mindfulness serve as transformative tools, not only mitigating stress but also fostering immune function and promoting the body's inherent healing abilities. Acknowledging and actively nurturing this intricate connection is a pivotal cornerstone in pursuing holistic health.

The interchange between emotional well-being and physical health is evident in various aspects of our lives. Chronic stress, often rooted in emotional strain, can manifest physically, contributing to ailments ranging from cardiovascular issues to compromised immune function. Conversely, physical conditions can affect mental health, mood, cognition, and overall emotional balance. Recognizing this interplay allows individuals to appreciate the holistic nature of health, where the mind and body function as an integrated and inseparable whole.

Practices such as meditation offer profound insights into the mind-body connection by providing a space for mental stillness and self-awareness. This ancient practice reduces stress and influences physiological processes, such as lowering blood pressure and promoting relaxation that positively impacts overall health. Similarly, yoga combines movement, breath, and mindfulness, offering a holistic approach that unifies the mind and body, promoting flexibility, strength, and emotional well-being.

Mindfulness, as a practice, emphasizes being present in the current moment. It encourages individuals to observe thoughts and emotions without judgment, fostering a deeper understanding of the mind-body connection. By cultivating mindfulness, individuals develop a heightened awareness of their internal states, allowing for a more conscious response to stressors and a greater sense of emotional balance.

The mind-body connection extends its influence beyond stress reduction to encompass immune function and healing. Scientific research supports the idea that positive emotional states can contribute to a strengthened immune system, while chronic stress may have the opposite effect. By embracing practices that enhance emotional well-being, individuals actively contribute to their body's defense mechanisms and its capacity to recover from illness.

Acknowledging and nurturing the mind-body connection is pivotal to achieving holistic health. This recognition transcends the dichotomy of mental and physical health, emphasizing their inseparability. A holistic health approach involves cultivating emotional resilience, adopting mindfulness practices, and engaging in activities that promote both psychological and physical well-being. By understanding this intricate connection, individuals empower themselves to make choices that contribute to a harmonious and balanced state of health. In this state, the mind and body collaborate to pursue overall well-being.

Navigating the realms of health and wellness constitutes a transformative journey of self-discovery and empowerment. It involves a multifaceted approach, harmonizing the understanding of the body's signals, seeking professional guidance, and embracing a holistic perspective. As individuals embark on this path, they weave together knowledge, intuition, and science to create a tapestry of comprehensive well-being. The synergy between medical interventions and holistic practices becomes the cornerstone of this journey, offering a holistic approach that nurtures the body, mind, and spirit. Individuals uncover the exquisite dance between science and intuition within this holistic exploration. In this delicate balance, informed choices and expert guidance converge to support a life of vitality, wellness, and profound self-awareness.

Understanding the body's signals is a foundational element in this journey. Every ache, every fluctuation in energy, and every emotional nuance serves as a message from the body. By tuning into these signals, individuals cultivate a heightened self-awareness that forms the basis for informed decision-making regarding their health. This practice of listening to the body fosters a deeper connection with its innate intelligence, providing insights into both the subtle whispers and the louder calls for attention.

Seeking professional guidance complements this self-awareness by tapping into the wealth of knowledge that medical experts bring. While the body communicates in its unique language, healthcare professionals offer a comprehensive understanding through the lens of scientific expertise. Regular check-ups, consultations, and diagnostic assessments become crucial elements in this collaboration, ensuring that individuals benefit from both their bodies' wisdom and medical professionals' insights.

Embracing a holistic perspective elevates the health and wellness journey to a more encompassing level. It recognizes the interconnectedness of physical, mental, and spiritual well-being. Holistic practices, ranging from mindfulness and nutrition to alternative therapies, are integral components of this approach. The synergy between medical interventions and holistic practices offers a comprehensive model that addresses symptoms and the underlying imbalances contributing to health issues.

Individuals discover the intricate dance between science and intuition within this holistic journey. Informed choices, grounded in scientific understanding, align with the intuitive wisdom that arises from a deep connection with the self. This dance allows individuals to navigate their health and wellness with a sense of empowerment, actively participating in decisions that resonate with their unique needs and values.

The result is a life of vitality, wellness, and profound self-awareness. The synergy between science and intuition, medical interventions and holistic practices, creates a harmonious approach to health that transcends the fragmented views of the body and mind. It becomes a holistic tapestry where the threads of knowledge and intuition weave together, supporting individuals in their journey toward optimal well-being. In this journey, the body, mind, and spirit dance in unison to the rhythm of a vibrant and flourishing life.

FAVORITE SONGS AND HYMNS OF COMFORT

Hymn: "I Am Weak, but Thou Art Mighty"

I am weak, but Thou art mighty; Hold me with Thy powerful hand. Bread of Heaven, Bread of Heaven, Feed me till I want no more; Feed me till I want no more.

Open now the crystal fountain, Whence the healing stream doth flow; Let the fiery, cloudy pillar Lead me all my journey through; Lead me all my journey through.

Strong Deliverer, strong Deliverer, Be Thou still my Strength and Shield; Be Thou still my Strength and Shield.

Lord, I trust Thy mighty power, Wondrous are Thy works of old; Thou deliver'st Thine from thralldom, Who for naught themselves had sold: Who for naught themselves had sold.

Thou didst conquer, Thou didst conquer, Sin, and Satan and the grave, Sin, and Satan and the grave.

When I tread the verge of Jordan, Bid my anxious fears subside; Death of death, and hell's destruction, Land me safe on Canaan's side; Land me safe on Canaan's side.

Songs and praises, songs and praises, I will ever give to Thee; I will ever give to Thee.

Hymn: "Jesus, Hold Me in the Palm of Your Hand"

Jesus, hold me in the palm of Your hand, Guiding me through life's shifting sand. When trials come and fears abound, In Your loving grip, I am found.

Though storms may rage and winds may blow, In Your embrace, I'm safe, I know. With You beside me, I'll never fear, For Your presence is always near.

Through valleys deep and mountains high, You're with me, Lord, by my side. In Your strong grasp, I find my rest, Assured that You know what's best.

When shadows fall and doubts arise, You're the Light that clears my skies. So, Jesus, hold me, never let me go, In Your love, I find peace and hope.

In the palm of Your hand, I'm secure, Your love is steadfast, strong, and pure. With every step, Your grace I'll see, Jesus, hold me for eternity.

Spiritual Baptist Version: "I See the Light House"

I see the light house, amen I see the light house, amen I see the light house shining in glory I see the light house, amen

I feel the spirit, amen I feel the spirit, amen I feel the spirit moving in glory I feel the spirit, amen

I hear the music, amen I hear the music, amen I hear the music ringing in glory I hear the music, amen

I touch the healing, amen I touch the healing, amen I touch the healing flowing in glory I touch the healing, amen

I know the Savior, amen I know the Savior, amen I know the Savior's love in glory I know the Savior, amen

I see the light house, amen I see the light house, amen I see the light house shining in glory I see the light house, amen

Song: "My God Is a Good God"

My God is a good God, yes He is My God is a good God, yes He is He woke me up and He turned me around And He planted my feet on higher ground

My God is a strong God, yes He is My God is a strong God, yes He is He lifted me up from the miry clay And He set my feet on the Rock to stay

My God is a kind God, yes He is My God is a kind God, yes He is He gave me peace in the midst of the storm And He keeps me safe in His loving arms

My God is a faithful God, yes He is My God is a faithful God, yes He is He never leaves me, He's always near He holds my hand and He calms my fear

My God is a good God, yes He is My God is a good God, yes He is He's my Savior, my Redeemer, my Friend And I'll praise His name till the very end

PRAYERS

The Power of Prayer and Opening Your Heart to Receive God's Wisdom

In the intricate tapestry of human existence, prayer is a profound connection between the finite and the infinite, the earthly and the divine. Through prayer, individuals open a channel of communication with a higher power, seeking solace, guidance, and transformation. Rooted in faith and humility, prayer holds within its essence the power to ignite change, cultivate inner strength, and invite the wisdom of the Creator into our lives.

A Gateway to Divine Guidance:

Prayer is more than mere words spoken into the void; it is a conversation with the Source of all wisdom and understanding. By approaching prayer with sincerity and an open heart, individuals create a sacred space to receive divine guidance. In the stillness of prayer, minds are stilled, distractions are set aside, and hearts become attuned to the whisper of God's voice. In this receptive state, one can truly grasp the depth of God's wisdom.

The Essence of Humility:

To open one's heart to receive God's wisdom is an act of profound humility. It acknowledges that human knowledge is limited and that a higher intelligence exists beyond our comprehension. In humility, individuals recognize their need for guidance beyond their understanding and lean on the wisdom of the Divine. This humility paves the way for a spiritual transformation, dismantling pride and opening the door to more significant insights.

Seeking the Path of Truth:

When one invites God's wisdom into their heart through prayer, they embark on a journey to uncover the path of truth. The world is often filled with noise, conflicting opinions, and distractions that cloud discernment. In seeking divine wisdom, one places a lantern on the path that leads to clarity, authenticity, and alignment with eternal truths. This wisdom is a compass guiding individuals through life's complexities and challenges.

Embracing a Higher Perspective:

God's wisdom transcends human limitations, offering a panoramic view of existence beyond time and space. Through prayer, individuals open themselves to receiving insights that are not bound by the constraints of the present moment. This higher perspective enables them to see beyond immediate circumstances, making decisions that are informed by a broader understanding of life's tapestry.

Nurturing Inner Transformation:

The process of opening one's heart to receive God's wisdom is a transformative journey. As wisdom is woven into the fabric of one's being, attitudes shift, priorities realign, and a more profound sense of purpose emerges. This inner transformation brings a renewed perspective on life, relationships, and personal growth. With each prayerful encounter, individuals become vessels of divine wisdom, radiating its light to the world around them.

Healing Prayers:

- Heavenly Father, I lift up those who are suffering from physical ailments. May Your healing touch bring restoration to their bodies and comfort to their hearts.

- Lord, I pray for emotional healing for those burdened by pain, grief, or anxiety. Surround them with Your peace that surpasses all understanding.
- Gracious God, I entrust those battling chronic illnesses to You. Strengthen their endurance, grant them relief, and guide their medical providers.
- Lord, bring healing to broken relationships and wounded hearts. May forgiveness and reconciliation mend what is torn.
- Merciful Savior, touch the minds of those facing mental health challenges. Grant them clarity of thought and the courage to seek help.

Courage Prayers:

- Heavenly Father, grant me the courage to face challenges with unwavering faith, knowing that You are my strength and refuge.
- Lord, instill courage in my heart to step outside my comfort zone, trusting that You will guide my path and provide for my needs.
- Gracious God, strengthen the resolve of those facing adversity. Help them stand firm in their convictions and overcome obstacles.

- Lord, grant me the courage to speak the truth in love and stand up for justice, even when it's difficult.
- Merciful Savior, empower me to face my fears with the knowledge that Your perfect love casts out all fear.

Wisdom Prayers:

- Heavenly Father, fill me with Your wisdom so I may discern the right path and make decisions aligned with Your will.
- Lord, grant me wisdom to navigate complex situations, seek advice from the wise, and make choices that honor You.
- Gracious God, bless me with wisdom in my relationships to communicate with grace and understanding.
- Lord, I ask for wisdom in my work and endeavors so that I may use my talents to make a positive impact.
- Merciful Savior, guide me in seeking wisdom from Your Word, that I may grow in spiritual understanding.

Enlightenment Prayers:

- Heavenly Father, illuminate my mind and heart with the truth of Your Word. Let Your light dispel any darkness in my life.
- Lord, open my eyes to see the beauty and blessings around me, even in challenging circumstances.

- Gracious God, grant me spiritual insight to discern Your guidance and recognize Your hand at work in my life.

- Lord, enlighten those who are lost or searching for meaning. Reveal Yourself to them in ways that resonate with their hearts.

- Merciful Savior, let Your divine wisdom shine brightly within me, leading me to a deeper understanding of Your ways.

Mercy Prayers:

- Heavenly Father, I humbly ask for Your mercy upon my shortcomings and mistakes. May Your grace cover my imperfections.

- Lord, extend Your mercy to those facing the consequences of their actions. Grant them opportunities for redemption.

- Gracious God, let Your mercy flow through me as I show compassion and forgiveness to others, just as You have shown to me.

- Lord, have mercy on those who are oppressed, suffering, or marginalized. May justice and compassion prevail in their lives.

- Merciful Savior, teach me to walk in mercy, offering love and understanding to all as a reflection of Your divine nature.

Children's Prayers:

"Gentle Jesus, Meek and Mild"

Gentle Jesus, meek and mild, Look upon a little child; Pity my simplicity, Suffer me to come to Thee.

Lamb of God, I look to Thee; Thou shalt my example be; Thou art gentle, meek, and mild; Thou wast once a little child.

Fain I would be as Thou art; Give me Thy obedient heart; Thou art pitiful and kind, Let me have Thy loving mind.

Loving Jesus, gentle Lamb, In Thy gracious hands I am; Make me, Savior, what Thou art, Live Thyself within my heart.

1. Guardian Angel Prayer:
Angel of God, my guardian dear, To whom God's love commits me here. Ever this day, be at my side, To light and guard, to rule and guide. Amen.

2. Armor of God Prayer:
Dear God, I put on the armor of faith to protect me throughout each day. With Your strength, I stand secure; guard me, Lord, forevermore.

3. God's Love Surrounds Me Prayer:

God, Your love surrounds me day and night like a blanket of warmth, keeping me safe and tight. I rest in Your care; no need to fear, for Your loving presence is always near.

4. Safe and Sound Prayer:

Dear God, as I sleep and when I wake, Keep me safe, my heart. You'll never forsake. In Your arms, I find my rest, Your love, and protection; I am blessed.

5. Shield of Faith Prayer:

God, wrap me in your shield of faith, Guard me against harm, and keep dangers at bay. With You beside me, I need not fear; Your love and protection are always near.

6. Nighttime Prayer for Protection:

Now I lay me down to sleep, I pray the Lord my soul to keep. Guide me through the night so deep; protect me, Lord, as Your love I reap.

7. Psalm 91 Prayer:

Heavenly Father, I dwell in Your shelter; beneath Your wings, I find sweet rest. You're my refuge, my fortress, and my protector; In You, I'm safe and truly blessed.

8. God's Watchful Eye Prayer:

God, like a shepherd watching over sheep, Keep me safe, my soul You'll always keep. Guide me in darkness, and in the light, I trust in Your love, day and night.

9. Prayer for a New Day:

Dear God, as a new day begins, Wrap me in Your love and keep me from sins. Guide my steps and protect my way. Thank You for this bright and blessed day.

10. Family and Friends Prayer:

God, bless my family and friends so dear; keep them safe, and bring them near. May Your love and protection always surround, In Your care, may they be found.

These prayers encompass a range of spiritual needs, from healing and courage to wisdom, enlightenment, and mercy. You can personalize and adapt these prayers to suit your circumstances and intentions. The power of prayer and opening one's heart to receive God's wisdom form a symbiotic relationship that shapes and enriches the human experience. Through the sacred channel of prayer, individuals invite the presence of the Divine into their lives, seeking guidance, understanding, and growth. As they humbly open their hearts, they create a receptive space for divine wisdom to flow, nurturing their souls and guiding them along the path of truth. In this beautiful dance of connection and transformation, the power of prayer and the reception of God's wisdom illuminate the journey of the human spirit.

SCRIPTURES OF ENCOURAGEMENT AND HEALING

Scriptures offer comfort, hope, and healing from the Bible. They serve as a source of strength during challenging times and a reminder of the God who cares for us deeply:

- **Comfort in Times of Trouble:** Many Scriptures provide assurances of God's presence and compassion in times of trouble. Psalm 34:17-18, for instance, highlights that God is near to those who are brokenhearted and saves those who are crushed in spirit. These verses remind us that we're not alone even when we face challenges; God is with us, offering comfort and solace.

- **Hope for Restoration and Healing:** The Scriptures also convey messages of hope for restoration and healing. Jeremiah 30:17 speaks of God's promise to restore health and heal wounds. These verses remind us that God can heal our physical, emotional, and spiritual wounds, offering us hope for a brighter future.

- **Divine Protection and Guidance:** Several Scriptures emphasize God's role as our protector and guide. Psalm 91:4 assures us that God's presence is like a shield, providing refuge and security. These verses remind us that even in times of uncertainty, we can trust in God's care and guidance.

- **Strength in Weakness:** Many Scriptures acknowledge human weakness but also highlight God's strength. 2 Corinthians 12:9 encourages us by reminding us that God's power is made perfect in our weaknesses. This offers us hope that God's strength can sustain us even when we feel inadequate or powerless.

- **Promises of Peace:** The Scriptures offer promises of peace amidst chaos and challenges. Isaiah 26:3 assures us that those who trust in the Lord will experience perfect peace. Philippians 4:6-7 speaks of a peace that transcends understanding, guarding our hearts and minds. These verses remind us that we can find peace in God's presence, regardless of external circumstances.

- **God's Provision and Care:** Several Scriptures highlight God's provision and care for His children. Psalm 23:1-4 paints a vivid picture of God as a shepherd who provides, guides, and comforts us. These verses remind us that God takes care of our needs and walks with us through difficult times.

- **The Source of Comfort and Healing:** These Scriptures remind us that God is the ultimate source of comfort and healing. Just as a loving parent cares for their child, God cares deeply for us. These verses assure us that we can turn to God in times of distress, finding solace in His presence and the promises of His Word.

- **Strengthening Faith and Resilience:** By meditating on these Scriptures, our faith is strengthened, and our resilience is deepened. They offer a foundation of hope that sustains us when facing adversity. We are reminded that God's love and faithfulness remain steadfast, empowering us to navigate challenges with courage and perseverance.

- **Encouragement to Trust God:** Above all, these Scriptures encourage us to trust God, no matter the circumstances. They remind us of God's character's unchanging nature and willingness to walk alongside us in our journeys. We can find comfort, hope, and healing even amid trials by trusting in His promises.

In essence, these Scriptures are like a wellspring of comfort and hope, offering us a lifeline to hold onto when life's challenges threaten to overwhelm us. They remind us that God's love is unwavering, His power is limitless, and His grace is sufficient for all our needs. Whether in moments of pain, uncertainty, or despair, these verses provide reassurance that we are not alone and can find strength in the arms of our loving Creator.

SCRIPTURES

- Psalm 34:17-18: "The righteous cry out, and the Lord hears them; he delivers them from all their troubles. The Lord is close to the brokenhearted and saves those who are crushed in spirit."

- Jeremiah 30:17: "But I will restore you to health and heal your wounds, declares the Lord."

- Exodus 15:26: "He said, 'If you listen carefully to the Lord your God and do what is right in his eyes, if you pay attention to his commands and keep all his decrees, I will not bring on

Scriptures of Encouragement and Healing

you any of the diseases I brought on the Egyptians, for I am the Lord, who heals you.'"

- Psalm 103:2-3: "Praise the Lord, my soul, and forget not all his benefits— who forgives all your sins and heals all your diseases."

- Isaiah 41:10: "So do not fear, for I am with you; do not be dismayed, for I am your God. I will strengthen you and help you; I will uphold you with my righteous right hand."

- Psalm 147:3: "He heals the brokenhearted and binds up their wounds."

- Matthew 11:28-30: "Come to me, all you who are weary and burdened, and I will give you rest. Take my yoke upon you and learn from me, for I am gentle and humble in heart, and you will find rest for your souls. For my yoke is easy and my burden is light."

- James 5:14-15: "Is anyone among you sick? Let them call the elders of the church to pray over them and anoint them with oil in the name of the Lord. And the prayer offered in faith will make the sick person well; the Lord will raise them up."

- Psalm 30:2: "Lord my God, I called to you for help, and you healed me."

- Isaiah 53:5: "But he was pierced for our transgressions, he was crushed for our iniquities; the punishment that brought us peace was on him, and by his wounds we are healed."

- Proverbs 17:22: "A cheerful heart is good medicine, but a crushed spirit dries up the bones."

- Matthew 9:35: "Jesus went through all the towns and villages, teaching in their synagogues, proclaiming the good news of the kingdom and healing every disease and sickness."

- Psalm 42:11: "Why, my soul, are you downcast? Why so disturbed within me? Put your hope in God, for I will yet praise him, my Savior and my God."

- Isaiah 40:31: "But those who hope in the Lord will renew their strength. They will soar on wings like eagles; they will run and not grow weary, they will walk and not be faint."

- Matthew 8:17: "This was to fulfill what was spoken through the prophet Isaiah: 'He took up our infirmities and bore our diseases.'"

Scriptures of Encouragement and Healing

- Psalm 30:5: "For his anger lasts only a moment, but his favor lasts a lifetime; weeping may stay for the night, but rejoicing comes in the morning."

- Psalm 91:4: "He will cover you with his feathers, and under his wings you will find refuge; his faithfulness will be your shield and rampart."

- 2 Corinthians 1:3-4: "Praise be to the God and Father of our Lord Jesus Christ, the Father of compassion and the God of all comfort, who comforts us in all our troubles, so that we can comfort those in any trouble with the comfort we ourselves receive from God."

- Psalm 73:26: "My flesh and my heart may fail, but God is the strength of my heart and my portion forever."

- Isaiah 26:3: "You will keep in perfect peace those whose minds are steadfast, because they trust in you."

- Psalm 46:1: "God is our refuge and strength, an ever-present help in trouble."

- 2 Corinthians 12:9: "But he said to me, 'My grace is sufficient for you, for my power is made perfect in weakness.' Therefore

I will boast all the more gladly about my weaknesses, so that Christ's power may rest on me."

- Psalm 91:9-10: "If you say, 'The Lord is my refuge,' and you make the Most High your dwelling, no harm will overtake you, no disaster will come near your tent."

- 1 Peter 5:7: "Cast all your anxiety on him because he cares for you."

- Psalm 138:7: "Though I walk in the midst of trouble, you preserve my life. You stretch out your hand against the anger of my foes; with your right hand you save me."

- Romans 15:13: "May the God of hope fill you with all joy and peace as you trust in him, so that you may overflow with hope by the power of the Holy Spirit."

- Psalm 55:22: "Cast your cares on the Lord and he will sustain you; he will never let the righteous be shaken."

- Isaiah 57:18-19: "I have seen their ways, but I will heal them; I will guide them and restore comfort to Israel's mourners, creating praise on their lips. Peace, peace, to those far and near," says the Lord. "And I will heal them."

- Philippians 4:6-7: "Do not be anxious about anything, but in every situation, by prayer and petition, with thanksgiving, present your requests to God. And the peace of God, which transcends all understanding, will guard your hearts and your minds in Christ Jesus."

- Psalm 23:1-4: "The Lord is my shepherd, I lack nothing. He makes me lie down in green pastures, he leads me beside quiet waters, he refreshes my soul. He guides me along the right paths for his name's sake. Even though I walk through the darkest valley, I will fear no evil, for you are with me; your rod and your staff, they comfort me."

LIVING THE BEATITUDES (MATTHEW 5:2-12): ANTOINETTE'S INSPIRATIONAL JOURNEY OF FAITHFUL SERVICE.

In the rich journey of Antoinette's life, every thread was woven with a purpose guided by the profound teachings encapsulated in the timeless words of the Beatitudes. As a faithful servant, she embraced these principles and allowed them to shape the fabric of her existence, creating an inspirational legacy of humility, compassion, and unwavering faith.

Blessed are the Poor in Spirit:

- Antoinette's spirit soared in its poverty, recognizing a wealth that transcended material possessions. In her humility, she opened her heart to the boundless richness of divine grace, finding solace in the kingdom of heaven even amidst life's temporal challenges.

Blessed are Those Who Mourn:

- Amidst the ebb and flow of life's sorrows, Antoinette emerged as a beacon of strength and comfort. Her compassion flowed like a gentle stream, offering solace to those navigating the stormy seas of grief. In her comforting presence, others found a harbor amid life's tempests.

Blessed are the Meek:

- Antoinette's meekness was a radiant strength—an inner calm that weathered life's storms gracefully. She navigated the world's complexities with a gentle spirit, leaving imprints of peace and serenity on the hearts she touched. In her meekness, she inherited the earth, not through conquest but through a quiet strength that shaped her surroundings.

Blessed are Those Who Hunger and Thirst for Righteousness:

- Antoinette's appetite for righteousness was insatiable, a hunger that fueled her commitment to justice and integrity. Her life was a testament to the belief that in pursuing righteousness, one finds satisfaction and a purpose that transcends the self.

Blessed are the Merciful:

- Mercy flowed from Antoinette like a perpetual spring, nourishing the parched landscapes of human need. Her healthcare profession, acts of kindness, and unwavering compassion were testaments to the transformative power of mercy—an echo of the divine mercy she sought and embodied.

Blessed are the Pure in Heart:

- Antoinette's heart, a sanctuary of purity, radiated authenticity. Her interactions were genuine, and her intentions were untainted by self-interest. In the purity of her heart, she found clarity—a lens through which she perceived the beauty in others and the world around her.

Blessed are the Peacemakers:

- As a peacemaker, Antoinette sowed seeds of harmony in a world often marred by discord. Her life became a testament to the transformative impact of fostering peace—whether mediating conflicts, offering a listening ear, or simply emanating tranquility in her presence.

Blessed are Those Persecuted for Righteousness' Sake:

- In the face of challenges and persecution, Antoinette stood resolute. Her commitment to righteousness was unwavering, and her perseverance in the face of adversity became a shining example of courage and faith. She bore the burdens of righteousness, knowing that the kingdom of heaven awaited those who endured.

Rejoice and be Glad:

- Amid life's challenges, Antoinette found cause for rejoicing. Her faith, firmly rooted in the teachings of the Beatitudes, allowed her to see beyond the temporal struggles. Each trial became a stepping stone, each setback an opportunity for growth. In rejoicing, she embraced the promise of a great reward—not measured in earthly accolades but in the eternal embrace of divine grace.

- Antoinette's journey, inspired by the Beatitudes, stands as a testament to the transformative power of faith, compassion, and unwavering commitment. Her life echoes the profound truth that in living out these principles, we find personal fulfillment and become instruments of inspiration for those who walk alongside us. Through her humble yet extraordinary journey, Antoinette invites us to embrace the Beatitudes as a guiding light—a path toward a life of purpose, love, and eternal joy.

CONTACT

For bookings, coaching group,
and individual sessions and general inquires.

Alicia Hurtt
alicia.hurtt@gmail.com
(301) 418-8819
PO Box 162
Hughesville, MD 20637

Made in the USA
Columbia, SC
03 August 2024